Brief Strategic
Problem-Solving Group Therapy
A Guide for Group Members

A Group Member's Guide to

Brief Strategic
Problem-Solving
Group Therapy

Making Group Therapy Work for You

By Terence T. Gorski

Based on the CENAPS Model

Adapted from *A Group Leader's Guide to Brief Strategic
Problem-Solving Group Therapy* with Pamela Woll

Herald House/Independence Press
Independence, Missouri

Terence T. Gorski, president
CENAPS Corporation
18650 Dixie Highway
Homewood, IL 60430
Phone: 708/799-5000; fax: 708/799-5032

Additional copies may be obtained from the publisher:
Herald House/Independence Press
3225 South Noland Road
P.O. Box 1770
Independence, MO 64055-0770
Phone: 1-800-767-8181 or 816/252-5010; fax: 816/252-3976

ISBN 0-8309-0733-5
Printed in the United States of America

99 98 97 96   1 2 3 4 5

Table of Contents

Part I

The Basics

In Problem-Solving Group Therapy you can:

1. Understand your problem more clearly

2. Learn the steps of problem solving in a safe, supportive, respectful environment

3. Identify and change:
    * mistaken thinking
    * unmanageable feelings
    * urges to do things that make life more painful
    * self-defeating behaviors
    * relationships that make problems worse

4. Be listened to, taken seriously, respected, and affirmed

5. Tap into the "master mind" or group conscience, a powerful source of knowledge, courage, strength, and hope in personal problem solving

CHAPTER 1

Welcome

Welcome to Brief Strategic Problem-Solving Group Therapy. If you're reading this book because you've decided to join a problem-solving group, congratulations! You've found the most advanced, most effective technique available. Don't worry, though: It may be advanced, but it's very easy to use, with clear guidelines and step-by-step directions.

Problem-Solving Group Therapy will help you understand your problem more clearly and learn the steps of problem solving in a safe, supportive, respectful environment. You'll learn how to identify and change mistaken thinking, unmanageable feelings, urges to do things that make life more painful, self-defeating behaviors, and ways of relating that make your problems worse.

In a group run on this model, people don't get away with game playing. It's not a good place to con or manipulate people for power or sympathy. But if you're serious about solving your problems—and willing to work hard and be honest—people will listen to you, take you seriously, respect you, and let you know they're on your side.

In a good group, the whole is really greater than the sum of its parts. When a group of people work together in harmony to reach a common goal or purpose, something special happens. A source of knowledge, courage, strength, and hope becomes available to each of the group members. This source is often called the "master mind" or group conscience. This source can be used as a powerful resource in personal problem solving.

Setting Your Goals in Problem-Solving Group Therapy

1. **Identify your target problem.**
   - The larger and deeper pattern of problems that surrounds the presenting problem (chemical dependency, mental or emotional problems, self-defeating personality styles, situational life problems)

2. **Decide on a goal for problem solving.**
   - Must be concrete—you can see, hear, or feel the result.

3. **Develop a step-by-step strategy for problem solving.**
   - Step 1: Problem identification and clarification
   - Step 2: Identification of alternatives and consequences
   - Step 3: Decision, action, and evaluation

CHAPTER 2

Setting Your Goals in Problem-Solving Group Therapy

Identify Your Target Problem

You've probably decided to enter group therapy because of a problem or issue that's been upsetting you or causing you pain. This issue is called your **presenting problem**. The presenting problem is important because it created the pain you needed in order to be willing to take action.

But this presenting problem is usually a small part of a larger pattern of problems. We become aware of the issue that hurts—like getting fired, being arrested, or having a relationship go bad. We often get hypnotized by our upset and pain and don't look at the true cause. This true cause is called a **core issue** or **target problem**.

For example, the presenting problem might be a pattern of painful and upsetting arguments with a loved one. What's causing these arguments? What is the core or central issue that most of the arguments revolve around? For some people it might be financial irresponsibility. What's causing them to be financially irresponsible? The answer to that question might be alcohol or drug abuse. When they're drinking or drugging they spend more money than they should. If they stopped drinking or drugging, they'd stop overspending. If they stopped overspending, the cause of the arguments would disappear and the fighting would stop.

Target Problems

Chemical Dependency
- problems with the abuse of alcohol or other mood-altering drugs that create painful or upsetting situations

Mental or Emotional Problems
- problems related to difficulty in thinking clearly, or difficulty in managing feelings and emotions, that cause painful or upsetting situations

Self-Defeating Personality Styles
- problems with the deeply rooted habits of thinking, feeling, acting, and relating to others that we learned as children, had reinforced as adolescents, and blindly act out as adults

Situational Life Problems
- problems in managing the acts of day-to-day living that can be caused either by overwhelming external events beyond our control or by problems with chemical dependency, mental or emotional problems, or self-defeating personality styles

Your therapist and the group will help you find the core issue that must be addressed if you're going to resolve your presenting problem once and for all. You'll be evaluated for chemical dependency so you can be sure your use of alcohol and drugs isn't causing your other problems or making them worse. You'll also be evaluated for **mental and emotional problems** like depression and anxiety. Your therapist and the group will also help you to look for **self-defeating personality traits** that might be causing or complicating your presenting problems.

These are just a few examples of target problems. There are many more. The first step in finding yours is to step back from your life, look at all the problems that are causing you trouble and pain, and find the larger problem that's at the center. Your group will help you do this.

Near the beginning of each session, the leader will ask which group members have problems they'd like to work on today. Most often these will be issues related to the problem-solving exercises that you're working on to solve your target problem. It's valuable to work on these issues in group, especially if you don't forget how they tie in with your target problem.

When you want to bring up or "present" a problem in group, it's a good idea to ask yourself how it relates to your target problem. Your first job will be to decide exactly what problem you want to work on and get a better understanding of it. Then you'll need to look at how this problem fits into your life. That way, you can make sure that this is the target or core issue that you want to work on in group.

Decide on Your Goals for Problem Solving

You'll get more out of group therapy if you know what you want from it. So once you've identified your target problem, it's time to set goals for problem solving. These goals don't have to be perfect, and they don't have to be final. But you need something to shoot for, something to hope for.

These goals should be "concrete"—you should be able to see, hear, or feel the results. If you can't, how will you know if you've reached your goals? A goal shouldn't be something loose and general like "get my life in order." How will you know your life is in order? What about your life will look, sound, or feel different? When you can answer those questions, you've found your goals.

Often your goals will include solutions to the kinds of troubles that led you into group. For example, the chemically dependent person described above might set these goals:

1. Stop drinking and using drugs. Attend recovery meetings five times a week and follow the advice I get there.

2. Get on my feet financially. Get and keep a job. Stop bouncing checks and start paying bills on time.

3. Improve my relationship with my family. Learn to communicate better and listen to what they say. Spend at least two nights a week just having fun with them.

Whatever your target problem is, you can find concrete goals. For example, if you have a habit of putting other people's needs first and ignoring your own, you might want to set goals like these:

1. Eat healthy food, get eight hours sleep a night, and exercise four times a week.

2. Spend at least an hour each day doing what I really want to do.

3. Learn to say "no" when people ask me to do things I'd resent doing.

Another example might be a person who has been court-ordered into therapy because of a problem with anger and getting into fights. That person might set goals like these:

1. Get off probation without any more arrests.

2. Stay out of fights, even if it seems like the other person is in the wrong.

3. Learn to relax when I think about the people and situations that I can't control, and instead think about things I can do something positive about.

Develop a Step-by-Step Strategy for Problem Solving

Once you have a problem and a goal, you need a strategy. Problem-Solving Group Therapy is set up to help you map out a strategy that will work for you. This strategy will be talked about in more detail in later chapters, but here's a quick introduction to the three steps of problem solving:

The Three Steps of Problem Solving

Step One: Problem Identification and Clarification

Step Two: Identification of Alternatives and Consequences

Step Three: Decision, Action, and Evaluation

Step One: Problem Identification and Clarification: Problem identification is simply figuring out what the real problem (the target problem) is and how it's affecting our lives. This isn't always easy. Sometimes it seems like everything is wrong and the group has to help us narrow it down. Or the real problem might be hidden under other problems—or under our fear of looking at our own part in it.

Problem clarification is the process of coming to understand the problem more clearly. The group has a whole series of questions it can ask to help clarify the problem. Some problems seem so big and confusing that we ignore all but the most obvious parts of them. That might seem comforting, but it actually makes problems more scary, because there's so much about them that's unknown. Problem clarification lets us know exactly what we're facing.

Step Two: Identification of Alternatives and Consequences: Alternatives are simply different choices we might make in trying to solve our problems. There's always more than one way to solve a problem. But if we've been stuck in the problem for a while, we might not realize that. We might have been trying the same thing over and over again and making things worse. The group process teaches us how to identify many alternative solutions.

Consequences are the results of our actions. Sometimes consequences are positive and pleasant. Sometimes they're destructive and painful. After we've found an alternative that we'd like to try, we need to think about the possible consequences it might bring. If we know ahead of time that the consequences will be painful in the long run, we can eliminate that alternative. Often we won't know, or we'll guess wrong. That's okay. What matters is that we practice the skill of thinking about consequences.

Step Three: Decision, Action, and Evaluation: A decision is when we choose an alternative to try. Our action is when we try it, in our lives or in a safe "practice" situation with somebody who knows we're just practicing. Our evaluation process involves looking honestly at what we did, how well we did it, and what happened as a result. That might lead us to try again, try another alternative, or even go back to problem clarification.

Of course, you won't go through all three steps in one session. It takes three to six sessions to go through the problem-solving process for one problem. The last section of this book gives all the information you'll need to get started in this. Meanwhile, it's time to start thinking about the biggest challenge in problem-solving group therapy: understanding and changing our thoughts, feelings, urges, actions, and relationships. The next chapter explains why this can be so hard, and why it's necessary for effective problem solving.

The Four Goals of Problem-Solving Group Therapy

1. **Change in Thinking:** Finding new ways to define our personal problems and figure out solutions:
    *   understanding our problems more clearly
    *   becoming aware of "self-talk"
    *   understanding our own "private logic"
    *   using images and "mental rehearsal"

2. **Change in Feeling:** Learning how to identify and change the emotions we experience when we think about our personal problems:
    *   learning to notice and identify our feelings
    *   building a language to express our feelings

3. **Change in Actions:** Doing something different to try to solve our problems:
    *   learning to choose actions that help our well-being
    *   learning to do things that will feel better later
    *   choosing not to act on self-defeating urges

4. **Change in Relating:** Finding new ways to involve other people in personal problem solving:
    *   noticing when people are contributing to our problems
    *   learning how to invite people to be part of our solutions
    *   getting comfortable with people who expect our best

CHAPTER 3

The Four Goals of Problem-Solving Group Therapy

If problems just "happened to us," then problem solving would simply be a process of learning to stay out of their way. But most of us take an active part in our problems, through the ways we think, feel, act, and relate to other people.

That's why changes in thinking, feeling, acting, and relating are called the four goals of Problem-Solving Group Therapy. Let's look at these goals one by one.

Change in Thinking

This is the first goal because our thoughts tend to drive our feelings, actions, and relationships. If we try to act differently but our thinking is still the same, we won't have much success. The three steps of problem solving pay a lot of attention to improving our thinking. For example, in problem identification and clarification we learn to think about the true nature of our problems and understand them more clearly—instead of getting caught up in excuses and side issues. In identifying alternatives and consequences we learn to see more options and predict the results of each option. Then we learn to think through the process of making decisions and to look honestly at what we've done to see how well it's worked.

In group we also become more aware of our "self-talk"—the conversation that goes on in our heads. We learn to tell which of the voices we "hear" are coming from the angry or hopeless part of us that tells us to do things that will hurt us. We also learn to identify and strengthen the voice of the reasonable, responsible part of our nature that wants our long-term well-being.

In group we also let others ask questions that help us understand our own **private logic**. That's the combination of beliefs and inner arguments that we use to solve problems. Sometimes our private logic can be way off base, and we need feedback from somebody outside the situation.

The problem-solving group also teaches us to use our imagination to look for solutions. We do this through the use of **images**, mental pictures that we create in our heads. When we use images in problem solving, they can help us understand and change in deeper and more powerful ways. Images can also be used for **mental rehearsal**, a way of imagining ourselves going through a situation so we'll be better prepared to handle it when it happens.

Change in Feeling

When we get into therapy many of us are out of touch with our emotions–"numbed off." Or else we're on "emotional overload." We experience intense and confusing feelings, and we tend to overreact. If we don't know or understand our feelings, we can't talk about them in a way people will understand. They get all jammed up inside us and cause us a lot of pain.

In group we learn to put honest and accurate word-labels on our feelings, so we know exactly what we're feeling. If we don't have the words to describe our feelings, the group gives us a whole set of words to pick from. We use those words to tell others what we're feeling. We also learn how to tell when it is and isn't safe to talk about our feelings.

In group we also learn to find the many connections between our thoughts and our feelings. This involves three things: (1) telling the difference between thoughts and feelings; (2) seeing how specific thoughts set off or trigger specific feelings; and (3) labeling and talking about these feelings so we don't have to act them out. An important step in managing unmanageable feelings is to learn to think different thoughts when it's not safe to feel the feelings that those thoughts usually trigger.

How I feel, and how strongly I feel that way (on a scale of one to ten):	
☐ Strong or ☐ Weak ___	☐ Safe or ☐ Threatened ___
☐ Angry or ☐ Caring ___	☐ Fulfilled or ☐ Frustrated ___
☐ Happy or ☐ Sad ___	☐ Proud or ☐ Ashamed, guilty ___

Change in Actions

In Problem-Solving Group Therapy we learn to tell the difference between **self-enhancing behaviors** (actions that are good for us) and **self-defeating behaviors** (actions that are bad for us). We learn that sometimes actions that feel good now—**immediate gratification**—will bring us trouble later, and sometimes actions that are hard or frustrating now will make our lives easier or better in the long run—**delayed gratification**.

For example, a newly recovering alcoholic in a stressful situation might have an urge to drink—a self-defeating behavior. She might decide instead to go to an AA meeting—a self-enhancing behavior. The drink might bring immediate gratification—good feelings while the first few drinks are going down. But the pain of returning to addictive drinking will soon set in. On the other hand, deciding not to have the drink might be frustrating and even emotionally painful at first. But when she has found the support needed to get through the crisis, the pain will pass. Then she'll have some satisfaction at having made a healthy decision and stayed sober.

Let's take another example: a man whose target problem is depression. He wakes up in the morning with the urge to turn off the alarm clock, roll over, and hide out in bed all day. This is a self-defeating urge. But instead of acting on it, he picks up the telephone and calls a friend or recovery sponsor and talks about how he's feeling. Then he forces himself to get up and get going even if he doesn't want to. These are self-enhancing behaviors that will help him solve the target problem of depression.

In group we learn that we can have urges to do self-defeating things, but we don't have to act on those urges. With the group's help we can build the courage to choose self-enhancing alternatives. We can practice these behaviors until they grow into habits. In time they actually become more attractive than the self-defeating choices. For example, an exercise program might seem at first like something simply to be endured—and avoided if possible. But after a while, when the body starts to feel stronger and more energetic, the exercises can be enjoyable, and we miss them if we're not able to do them.

Change in Relating

In Problem-Solving Group Therapy we learn to relate to people and situations in more positive and productive ways. We learn and practice skills that help us communicate more clearly and effectively. We become more honest and more cooperative because it's safe to do that.

We also start looking for and noticing which of the people in our lives are *enabling* our self-defeating behaviors, or making it easier for us to do things that will hurt us in the long run. Sometimes these people make excuses for us or ignore the ways we're hurting ourselves. Sometimes they go to the other end of the scale, telling us we're worthless and we'll never amount to anything. Either way, they make it easier for us not to try to get better.

In group we learn to work with these people to help them stop doing the things that help us keep our problems going. We also work on getting more comfortable with people who have higher standards for our behavior, and who hold us to those standards.

There are many kinds of problems and many ways the group experience can help people tackle those problems. As you read this book and plunge into the group experience, you'll see how Problem-Solving Group Therapy is set up to give you the tools you need to become part of the solution instead of part of the problem. Life can be counted on to bring challenges and pain from time to time. The least we can do is to be on our own side and develop the thoughts, feelings, actions, and relationships that will support our long-term well-being.

Responsibilities of Group Members

As a group member you are responsible for:

1. Giving a reaction to last session by telling the group:
   - your level of stress since the last group session
   - your level of functioning since the last group session
   - what you thought about last group
   - how you felt about last group
   - the three group members who stood out to you and why

2. Completing and reporting on assignments to help you make progress in problem solving.

3. Presenting problems to the group at least once every third group session.

4. Listening to other group members, telling them what you heard them say, and asking if you understood correctly.

5. Asking clarifying questions when other group members are presenting problems.

6. Giving feedback to members who are working on problems by saying what you think their problem is and how you feel about them as a person.

7. Completing the closure exercise by reporting the most important thing you learned in session and what you intend to do differently as a result.

CHAPTER 4

Responsibilities of Group Members

By now you're probably wondering how all this work gets done in group. Basically it's the group members who do the work, not the group leader. The leader is there to act as: (1) a **leader**, by showing you what needs to be done; (2) a **teacher**, by showing you how to do it; and (3) a **coach**, by watching you do it and giving you feedback and suggestions about how to improve.

Expectations

There are seven responsibilities that each group member has. If you're going to work in this kind of group, all of these responsibilities are yours. They aren't optional—you can't "take them or leave them," any more than you can "take or leave" a job responsibility that you don't enjoy. They're part of the price of learning to solve life problems in this very effective way.

The group responsibilities will be covered more completely later in this book, but here's a quick overview:

1. Reactions to last session: At the beginning of each group session you'll be asked and expected to report to the group on five things: your level of stress since last session; your level of functioning since last session; what you thought about the last session; how you felt about the last session; and the three group members who stood out to you and why they stood out. You'll also be asked to rate your level of stress and level of functioning since the last session. More about this in chapter 8, "Reactions to Last Session."

2. Completing and reporting on assignments: When you work on a problem in group, the group leader might ask you to carry out an assignment that will help you make progress on that problem. This might be something to write, someone to talk to, a new action to try, etc. Your problem must be clearly defined, and the assignment must be designed to help you solve the problem. You'll be expected to work seriously on these assignments, complete them in a timely manner, and report to the group on what you learned by completing them.

3. Presenting problems to the group: In order to qualify for Problem-Solving Group Therapy you need to have problems that you're willing to bring before the group. At the beginning of each session the group will be asked who has a problem that they'd like to work on in group. You'll be expected to present a problem to the group at least once every third session. Most of the time these problem presentations will be about the steps in the action plan you're using to solve your target problem. At other times you might present a new problem or crisis situation that has just come up and needs attention.

4. Listening when others present problems: When others are presenting their problems you'll be expected to pay attention and get involved in the problem-solving process. This means really listening when others are talking about their problems, telling them what you heard them say, asking them if you understood what they said, and listening to their answers.

5. Asking clarifying questions: When others have presented their problems, you'll be expected to ask at least two or three intelligent and relevant questions designed to help them understand their problems more clearly. "Intelligent" means your questions make sense. "Relevant" means they're related to helping the problem presenter solve the target problem. This is part of the clarification process described earlier. You'll also be expected to ask questions that will help them think of possible solutions. Your questions must be well thought out and appropriate for the problem being discussed.

6. Giving feedback: When other group members have presented their problems, and the clarifying questions have been asked and answered, you'll be expected to tell them two things: what you think the real nature of their problem is; and how you feel about them as people. For the safety of all group members, this feedback must be in line with the group rules outlined in the next chapter.

7. Completing the closure exercise: At the end of each session you'll be expected to do a closure exercise. First you complete an exercise form that the leader hands out to the group; then you briefly tell the group about your answers to the questions on the form. Basically, this exercise asks you to look at and report the most important thing you learned during the session, what you intend to do differently as a result, the assignment you're working on, how stressful you feel, and how well you're doing in group.

That's it. Those are your responsibilities. As in many other situations, you'll find that the benefits you get will be equal to the effort you've put into it. And again, this isn't just about solving the problems you bring into group. It's also about learning new ways of thinking, feeling, acting, and relating. These responsibilities form a structure that helps you learn and practice these new ways. But every group member has to fulfill all of these responsibilities, or it stops feeling fair to the other members.

The next chapter looks at another structure: the rules that make the group a safe place to show up; be honest; and share thoughts, feelings, and experiences. As you read it, please start to think about how those rules might keep you safe as you work to carry out your group responsibilities.

Basic Rules for Group Members

1. **Punctuality and Attendance:** Attend all sessions and be on time.

2. **Compliance with Basic Responsibilities:** Comply with all seven responsibilities.

3. **Freedom of Participation:** Within the group rules, you can say anything, but others can give you feedback.

4. **Right of Refusal:** Within the group responsibilities, you can refuse to do things that trigger uncomfortable feelings, but others can give you feedback.

5. **Confidentiality:** Don't discuss other group members' words or actions with anyone outside the group.

6. **No Violence:** Physical or verbal violence, and/or the threat of violence, can be grounds for dismissal from group.

7. **No Dating, Romantic Involvement, or Sexual Involvement:** These activities can hurt you and your treatment. Bring any involvement to the group or your counselor at once.

8. **Communication before Termination:** If you decide to leave group, tell the group in person before you leave.

CHAPTER 5
Group Rules

If trust were easy, and respect came naturally to all of us, we wouldn't need basic ground rules for Problem-Solving Group Therapy. Many of us wouldn't need therapy at all! But we live in the real world, where in many situations it isn't safe or appropriate to speak openly about the problems that are causing pain and trouble in our lives. That's why it's so important that the group therapy experience have a strong rule structure that makes it a safe and respectful place for all group members.

Here's a quick rundown of the rules:

1. Punctuality and Attendance

You're expected to show up for all group sessions, get there on time, and stay until the end of the session. If you miss sessions, you might be asked to leave the group. If you show up late, your group leader might handle the situation in one of two ways, depending on the setting in which your therapy is taking place. In some settings you might not be allowed to stay for the session. In others you might be asked to tell the group why you're late and develop an action plan that will help you be on time in the future. If you miss a session without getting permission first, you won't be able to attend another session until you've made and kept an appointment with the leader to talk about why you didn't show up.

These rules are necessary to show respect for the group members who do show up on time and participate at each session. They make the group a dependable environment, so that each person can count on seeing the others at each session. But these rules are also necessary to protect group members from the temptation to "escape" the group process just when it's bringing up some scary emotions. The only way to get better is to go through those emotions and out the other end. If you try to back out of it, the pain won't go away.

2. Compliance with Basic Responsibilities

When you "sign up" to be a group member, your agreement to do that means that you're willing to fulfill all of the seven basic group responsibilities described in the previous chapter. If you were allowed to pick and choose from the responsibilities, the group process wouldn't work as well as you need it to work. It would be a waste of your time, and of the group's time.

3. Freedom of Participation

You'll be expected to stick to the standard format and basic responsibilities. Beyond that, though, you can say anything you want any time you want to say it. Other group members have the right to give you their reactions or feedback about what you say and how you say it. This way, you won't feel like you have to "stuff" your thoughts and feelings inside you. But the other group members will hold you responsible for what you say.

Silence isn't considered a virtue in this group. Silence can actually work against the success of the group therapy process—both for the person who should speak out and for the people who would benefit from hearing what that person says.

4. Right of Refusal

You can't get away with refusing to carry out the basic group responsibilities, but you can refuse to answer any question or complete any assignment. The other group members can't force you to participate, but they do have the right to tell you how they feel about your silence or your choice not to get involved. This gives you a way to protect your safety when you've been asked to say or

do things that you feel would be unsafe. It also keeps you account-
able to the rest of the group.

5. Confidentiality

You're not allowed to talk outside the group setting about what
any other group members have said or done in group. They're not
allowed to talk about what you've said or done. This rule holds
true even if the outside person you're talking to is very trust-
worthy or has never met the group member you're talking about.
This rule is absolutely necessary to protect the safety of each group
member. It helps create a setting in which people can trust one
another enough to say what they really mean.

Your group leaders are allowed to talk about what goes on in
group with other members of the treatment team. This is sometimes necessary so they can provide more effective help. They can
also report any actions that are out of line, or any violation of
rules and responsibilities. There are also certain kinds of actions—
child abuse, for example—that group leaders are required by law to
report if they hear about them. This is called **mandatory reporting**. If you're not sure how this works, ask your group leader to
explain it to you.

6. No Violence

If you use any physical or verbal violence in the group, you
might be asked to leave the group permanently. Physical violence
includes pushing, shoving, or hitting other group members. Verbal
violence includes making threats, yelling, using swear words, and
name calling. Threatening to do something violent is just as serious a violation of this rule as actually doing it. The "no violence"
rule also applies to any contact you might have with group leaders
or members outside the group setting. Whether it's physical or
verbal, violence destroys trust. A group loses its effectiveness if
trust is destroyed.

7. No Dating, Romantic Involvement, or Sexual Involvement

Dating, romantic involvement, and sexual involvement are not allowed among group members. These kinds of activities can ruin the effectiveness of one or both members' treatment. They can leave one or both members in worse shape than they were when they started treatment. And, of course, there can be no dating and romantic or sexual involvement between a group leader and a group member.

If any of these kinds of involvement start to develop, it's your responsibility to tell the group, the group leader, or your individual counselor at once. If anyone is even flirting or trying to start involvement with you or with someone else in the group, it needs to be reported. Everyone's success in learning to problem-solve is much more important than sexual or romantic attraction. If two group members are really right for each other, they'll wait until after their full term in group has ended.

8. Communication before Termination

Anyone who decides to leave the group before the agreed-upon number of sessions has a responsibility to inform the group in person before leaving. This protects group members from the confusion and negative feelings that we sometimes get when people simply "disappear" from our lives without an explanation. When group members have grown to care about one another, they care about the changes in each person's life. They deserve to know why a group member is leaving, and to have a chance to tell the group how they feel about it.

All these rules have a common purpose: to protect the right of each member to be respected, feel safe, and have an effective group therapy experience. The next chapter will tell you how these rules are protected.

Corrective Procedures

If you fail to meet group responsibilities, or if you violate group rules, here are the steps your group leader will take:

Step 1: The Verbal Warning:

- You'll be told that you're violating group rules or not meeting your responsibilities and asked if you see the problem and are willing to work at correcting it. If you're not willing, you should voluntarily leave the group.

Step 2: Group Problem Solving and Feedback:

- If you continue to have a problem with the rules or responsibilities, you'll be asked to work on this problem in group. You'll use the standard problem-solving process to make it possible to fulfill all rules and responsibilities.

Step 3: Suspension or Termination from Group:

- If you still can't or won't comply with the basic rules and responsibilities, you won't be allowed to continue in group. Your leader will help you find a more appropriate way to get the help you need.

These steps are necessary to protect each group member's right to respect, safety, and an effective group therapy experience.

CHAPTER 6

Corrective Procedures

We all know that a set of rules and responsibilities will make a difference only if there are clear and reliable consequences for not following them. In Problem-Solving Group Therapy, we aren't forced to follow the rules and responsibilities. The group experience is all about understanding that we have many alternative choices, and each choice has its consequences. This chapter is about the consequences of breaking the rules outlined in the last two chapters.

People who break rules in group aren't "punished" as if they were "bad."A rule violation (breaking a rule or not carrying out a responsibility) is treated as a problem to be solved, using all of the skills and methods of problem solving.

There are three steps that group leaders take if group members break the rules: (1) leaders point the problem out in group **(the verbal warning)**; (2) if members continue to break the rules, these violations become problems to be solved in group **(group problem-solving and feedback)**; and (3) if group members are still breaking the rules, those members are asked to leave group, either for a while or permanently **(suspension or termination from group)**. Here's a little more information about each of these steps:

Step 1: The Verbal Warning

This takes place the first time a rule is broken. When these violations occur, group leaders point out the violations in group. They ask the members who broke the rules if they recognize the problems and are willing to correct them. Sometimes group leaders will schedule individual sessions with members who have broken the rules. This might be because the leaders think there may be a misunderstanding or a deeper problem behind the violation.

Step 2: Group Problem Solving and Feedback

If members continue to break the rules after Step 1, they're asked to talk about their inability to follow the rules or responsibilities. They do this in the same way they'd present any other problem to be solved. The groups then follow the standard problem-solving process. This step is usually successful in helping members follow the rules and fulfill their responsibilities.

Step 3: Suspension or Termination from Group

If group members are still breaking the rules after Steps 1 and 2, they can't be allowed to stay in group. This is necessary if they simply *won't* follow the rules, or if they truly *can't* follow the rules. In either case, their actions would threaten the feelings of safety, respect, and cooperation that are needed to create an effective problem-solving group. In these cases group leaders might decide to "suspend" these members—ask them to leave the group until they're willing to follow the rules of the group. Or group leaders might refer these members to another kind of therapy or treatment that's more appropriate for them, and end or "terminate" their working relationship with the group.

Group members who break the rules will not be abandoned, though. The leader will help them find a kind of counseling or therapy in which they'll be willing and able to participate.

Membership in a problem-solving group comes at a price. The price includes a willingness and ability to carry out the basic responsibilities and rules. Most group members have little or no trouble doing this, although at times they might not feel like doing it. They come to understand that they have a lot to gain by learning this way of problem solving. It's worth pushing themselves a little and taking some risks. And the group is there to support them through it all.

Part II

The Group Therapy Structure

Problem-Solving Group Therapy: Standard Agenda

1. **Preparation:** Between sessions, members complete assignments and prepare reactions to the last session.

2. **Opening Procedure:** Introductions, check-in, and centering technique (relaxation and mental review of last session and what happened since).

3. **Reactions to Last Session:** Levels of stress and functioning since last session, what you thought and felt about last session, and the three members who stood out to you and why.

4. **Report on Assignments:** Target problem, assignment for solving the target problem, assignment status, and time needed to work on it.

5. **Setting the Agenda:** Members volunteer to work and briefly explain what they want to work on.

6. **Problem-Solving Process:** Problem presentation, questioning, feedback, and summary and assignment.

7. **The Closure Exercise:** Most important thing learned in group, what you're going to do differently as a result, and your current assignment.

8. **Review and Evaluation:** An after-the-session review of progress, problems, and personal reactions to the session.

CHAPTER 7

The Group Therapy Agenda: A Quick Look

This chapter is a short introduction to the agenda that's used for each Problem-Solving Group Therapy session. The rest of this section goes into more detail on the two agenda items that begin and end the problem-solving process: Reactions to Last Session and the Closure Exercise. Items 4 and 6—Report on Assignments and Problem-Solving Group Process—are discussed in Part III, Solving Problems in Group Therapy. But first, here's the quick overview:

1. Preparation

This takes place outside the group setting, before each session. Group members prepare for the session by thinking about their target problem, the steps they're using to solve it, the assignment they're working on, and their reactions to the last session.

2. Opening Procedure

The group leader (or leaders) make sure all members are seated so they can see one another. The leader introduces any new group members and takes attendance. Then the group leader leads an exercise that helps members relax, notice their thoughts and feelings, remember what happened in the last session, and remember which group members stood out to them and why.

3. Reactions to Last Session

Each group member gives a two-minute reaction to the last session by completing five statements: (1) "I rate my level of stress since last session as..."; (2) "I rate my level of functioning since last session as..."; (3) "What I thought about the last group session is..."; (4) "How I felt about the last group session is..."; and (5) "The three group members (other than the leaders) who stood out to me from last session are...and the reasons they stood out are...".

When they give their reactions, group members talk directly to the people they are reacting to, instead of talking *about* them. An example would be: "John, you stood out to me because you were able to challenge the group leader. I would have been to afraid to do that, and I respect you for it."

4. Report on Assignments

Each group member gives a brief answer to each of these questions: (1) What is the target problem you're trying to solve? (2) What assignment are you working on to try to solve it? (3) What did you want to accomplish by working on this assignment? and (4) Did you complete the assignment? If so, do you want time to work on the results in group? If not, why not and when will it be done? Each group member's report should take no more than two minutes.

5. Setting the Agenda

The leader sets the agenda by asking, "Who has an issue to work on in group?" Group members who have assignments or new problems that they'd like to work on tell the leader so at this time. The group leader then requests a short (thirty-second) description of the problem and asks if this is an emergency issue that must be dealt with immediately. The leader uses that information in deciding which problems will be on the agenda for the session and in what order. Group members who don't have time to present their problems in this session will be first on the agenda in the next.

6. Problem-Solving Group Process

This process has four steps: (1) **Problem Presentation**, a general description or identification of the problem or assignment; (2) **Questioning by the Group**, a process that helps the whole group clarify the problem and understand the thoughts, feelings, actions, and relationships involved; (3) **Feedback from Group Members** to get more information about the problem and the group members' feelings about it; and (4) **Summary and Assignment by the Group Leader**. In this step the leader first gives a summary of the group's feedback. Then the leader helps the problem presenter develop an assignment that will help the process to the next step of problem solving.

7. Closure Exercise

The group leader hands out copies of a **Session Documentation Form** and gives the members time to fill it out. That form asks the group members to identify their target problems and describe the most important thing that will help them solve their target problem. Then it asks what they're going to do differently as a result of what they've learned, and asks about the assignments they've agreed to work on. There are also several questions that ask participants to rate their involvement in group. After they've filled these out, each member has about two minutes to read the answers to the group. Then the group leader writes a note at the bottom of each member's worksheet.

8. Review and Evaluation

After each session group members are encouraged to think about what happened in group, the progress each member has made, how they feel about the session, etc.

Reactions to Last Session

1. **I rate my level of stress since last session as...and the reason I rated it that way is....**
    On a scale of 1-10:
    *   low = 0-3
    *   moderate = 4-6
    *   severe = 7-10
    at 7 we "space out"
    at 8 we get defensive
    at 9 we overreact
    at 10 we can't function and can get violent

2. **I rate my level of functioning since last session as...and the reason I rated it that way is....**
    On a scale of 1-10:
    *   normal functioning = 7-10
    *   mild impairment of functioning = 5-6
    *   moderate impairment of functioning = 3-4
    *   severe impairment of functioning = 1-2

3. **What I thought about the last group session is....**

4. **How I felt about the last group session is....**

5. **The three group members (other than the leaders) who stood out to me from last session are...and the reasons they stood out are....**

    For questions 3, 4, and 5:
    *   Breathe deeply, and notice your thoughts and feelings.
    *   Use statements like "I think..." and "I feel...".
    *   Use first-person "I" statements.
    *   Talk directly to the person and make eye contact.

CHAPTER 8

Reactions to Last Session

Each group session starts with an exercise called "Reactions to Last Session." At this time each group member must give a reaction. That's one of your responsibilities. If you don't, you may not be allowed to stay for the group session. So it's important that you think about your reactions to the last session before you come to group, and get ready to talk about them.

This exercise is designed to help you to remember what happened in the last group session and what you've done differently since then. That's so you can bring what you learned—and the changes in your behavior—with you into this session. There's a saying that often proves true: Therapy is what happens *between* sessions.

Reactions will also help you get connected with the other group members and "warm up" before the problem-solving work begins. This will help you feel more comfortable presenting problems, asking questions, and giving feedback.

A reaction consists of five sentences that you'll complete: (1) "I rate my level of stress since last session as..."; (2) "I rate my level of functioning since last session as..."; (3) "What I thought about the last group session is..."; (4) "How I felt about the last group session is..."; and (5) "The three group members (other than the leaders) who stood out to me from last session are...and the reasons they stood out are...".

Review each of these five parts so that you know exactly what's expected of you, and exactly how to give a good reaction. Let's take the five reaction questions one by one:

I rate my level of stress since last session as...and the reason I rated it that way is....

In group you'll learn how to rate your stress level on a scale of one to ten, then tell the group your score. If your stress level is **low**, you score from 0 to 3. That means you have only the normal stress of day-to-day living and manage that stress well. It doesn't cause any painful feelings for you.

If your stress level is **moderate**, you score from 4 to 6. You feel a lot of stress and sometimes don't manage it well. It causes painful feelings, but it doesn't lead you to do things that create more problems in your life.

If your stress level is **severe**, you score from 7 to 10. You feel way too much stress and usually don't manage it well. It causes painful feelings for you, and you find yourself doing things that create more problems in your life.

At a score of 7 on this scale, you "space out" or have a hard time holding onto thoughts. At a score of 8, you get defensive or want to argue or strike out at people if they appear to be challenging you. At a score of 9, you overreact—your reactions to people and events are way out of line. At a score of 10, you can't "function"— can't do the basic things you need to do to get along and survive.

After you rate your level of stress, you'll need to tell the group why you rated your stress that way. For example, you might say: "I rate my level of stress since last session as a six. A few stressful things have happened, but I think I've handled them well. So I rate my stress at the high end of the moderate range."

I rate my level of functioning since last session as...and the reason I rated it that way is....

In group you'll also learn to rate your level of functioning on a ten-point scale. This scale will help you rate how well you've taken care of yourself and your responsibilities, gotten along with people, etc. In the stress scale a lower score means you feel better, because it means you have a lower level of stress. In the level of functioning scale it's the opposite. A higher score means you feel better, because it marks a higher level of functioning. There's often a connection between stress and functioning: As stress goes up, functioning goes down.

If you have **normal functioning**, you score somewhere from 7 to 10 on the Level of Functioning Scale. You have no serious symptoms or signs of trouble. Your stress is normal, you feel good, and you function well.

If you have **mild impairments in functioning**, you score from 5 to 6. Your symptoms of trouble are annoying, but you can manage them if you put out more effort. Because you're working harder to manage your symptoms, you're avoiding any serious problems at work, at school, or in your relationships.

If you have **moderate impairments in functioning**, you score from 3 to 4. Your symptoms sometimes cause trouble in your life even though you're putting out more effort to manage them. You're having serious problems at work, at school, or in your relationships with people.

If you have **severe impairments in functioning**, you score from 1 to 2. Your symptoms almost always cause problems in your life. You aren't able to get along or take care of your basic needs and responsibilities. You don't believe there's any hope. You might feel like hurting or killing yourself or someone else, or you lose the ability to take care of yourself.

You can probably see why it's important to tell the group about your stress and functioning. Now here are sample answers to the last three questions:

· *What I thought about the last group session is....* This part of the "Reactions" exercise is a statement of your thoughts about last session—your opinions about it, the things you learned, etc. One example: "I thought last week's group was very productive. I learned a lot about how I deal with anger and frustration. There was a lot of good feedback when I talked about my problem."

· *How I felt about the last group session is....* In this statement you get away from thoughts and into your feelings about the last session. You'll need to say more than "I felt good" or "I felt bad." It's important to tell the group the specific feelings you've been having—happy or sad, angry or caring, proud or ashamed, safe or threatened, etc. If it's hard to pinpoint your feelings, you can use the Feelings Chart on page 21. Here's an example of a feeling statement: "I had a feeling of accomplishment as I worked on my problems. I was surprised. I got excited instead of depressed for the first time in a long time. I felt happy, proud, and pleased with myself!"

The three group members (other than the leaders) who stood out to me from last session are...and the reasons they stood out are....

It's important to quickly connect with the people who stood out to you from last session. This forces you to get out of yourself and think about others. It also lets others know they said or did something that was noticed by others.

Here's an example: "Joe, you stood out to me because you understood what I was talking about. Mary, you stood out because you told me that you cared about me. I'm not sure if I believe you—if you were being honest or just saying what you thought I wanted to hear. Pete, I was upset with you because you didn't seem to pay attention to me when I was talking. A lot of people do this to me and I generally ignore it. But I'm supposed to try new things in group, so I decided to tell you and see what would happen."

When you give reactions, take time to breathe and notice your thoughts and feelings. You can talk about them, too. In reporting thoughts, start with the words "I think." For feelings, start with the words "I feel." When you give feedback to others, look straight at them and make eye contact. Talk in the first person, using the word "you" instead of "he," "she," or "they."

46

There are no right or wrong reactions. At times they might be incomplete or in the wrong format, but your thoughts and feelings are valid. These reactions might not take up much time, but they're a powerful tool in problem solving.

The Closure Exercise

1. **My target problem is....**

   This is the central problem or core issue you're in group to address.

2. **The most important thing I learned in group to help me solve my target problem is....**

   This is something you've heard or discovered that might serve as a key to the target problem.

3. **What I'm going to do differently as a result of what I learned is....**

   This is something concrete and "doable" that you can put into practice right away.

4. **The assignment I'm working on to solve my target problem is....**

   This is the assignment you've worked out with the group leader.

5. **I rate my level of stress as....**

   Using the stress scale, 0–3 = low; 4–6 = moderate; 7–10 = high stress.

6. **I rate my level of functioning as....**

   Using the Level of Funcioning Scale, 7–10 = normal functioning; 5–6 = mild impairment; 3–4 = moderate impairment; 1–2 = severe impairment.

7. **My problem-solving stage is....**

   Stage 1 = Problem Identification and Clarification; Stage 2 = Identification of Alternatives and Consequences; Stage 3 = Decision, Action, and Evaluation.

8. **I rate my level of motivation as....**

   Rate your motivation on a scale from 1 to 10.

9. **I rate my level of involvement as....**

   Rate your functioning on a scale from 1 to 10.

10. **I rate my level of satisfaction as....**

    Rate your satisfaction on a scale from 1 to 10.

CHAPTER 9

The Closure Exercise

The Closure Exercise is there to help you pinpoint the most important things you've learned in session and how you think they might affect your life. It completes the process started in the Reactions to Last Session and helps prepare you for the work you'll be doing between sessions.

About fifteen minutes before the end of each group, the leader will pass out copies of the Session Documentation Form shown on page 50. Group members are given a few minutes to fill out their sections of these forms. The top half of the form—Client Notes—asks group members to: (1) identify their target problem; (2) describe the most important thing they learned in the day's session to help them solve the target problem; (3) tell what they're going to do differently as a result of what they've learned; and (4) describe the assignment they're working on to solve their target problem. Group experience has shown that writing these things down right after a session helps group members learn more and put it to better use in their lives.

On the bottom half of the form—Rating Scales and Notes—both the group member and the group leader have a chance to record how the member is doing. Except for the "Problem-Solving Stage" (question 7), all of these scores run on a scale from one to ten (question 7 follows the problem-solving steps outlined in chapter 10). When you report your score to the group, don't just tell them the number. Briefly tell them why you chose that number.

Session Documentation Form

Developed By Terence T. Gorski (© Copyright, Terence T. Gorski, 1985, 1992, 1995)

Client: _____ Therapist: _____

Type: ❑ Group ❑ Individual ❑ Psychoeducation ❑ Family ❑ Other: _____

Day/Date/Time: _____

Part 1: Client Notes

1. My target problem is: _____

2. The most important thing I learned in this session to help solve the target problem is:

_____

_____

3. What I am going to do differently as a result of what I learned is:

_____

_____

4. The assignment I am working on to solve my target problem is:

_____

_____

Client Signature: _____ Date: _____

Part 2: Rating Scales and Notes

Person Completing the Rating	Self	Leader
5. Stress Score:		
6. The Level of Functioning Outside of Sessions Score:		
7. Problem Solving Stage:		
8. Problem Solving–Motivational Response Score:		
9. Session Involvement Score:		
10. Client Satisfaction Rating:		

Therapist's Progress Note:

_____

_____

_____

_____

Therapist's Signature: _____ Date: _____

Copies available from CENAPS, 18650 Dixie Hwy, Homewood, IL 60430 (phone: 708/799-5000).

After all group members have filled out their sections of the form, they have a chance to talk to the rest of the group about what they've written. As each group member speaks, the leader writes a comment in the Therapist's Progress Note section of that member's form, then tells the member what's been written there. The group member keeps a copy of the completed form.

The Closure Exercise helps "tie up" the lessons learned in each group session, but the work doesn't stop there. It's important to think back on the group session each day and use what you've learned in your day-to-day life. It's useful to keep a journal where you can write down what you've learned and how you applied it to solving your problems.

If the group as a whole can get together after the session to talk about the experience, that also can make the group process more effective. You can go out for coffee as a group and have an informal review and evaluation session. Sometimes these "sessions after the sessions" are just as helpful as the session itself—or even more so.

Now that you've read a little about the reaction and closure exercises that begin and end the group's problem-solving work, it's time to look in much more detail at the problem-solving process itself. The last section of this book is all about that process.

Part III

Solving Problems in Group Therapy

The Three-Step Problem-Solving Strategy

1. **Problem Identification and Clarification:**
   In Step 1, group members help problem presenters determine the nature of their target problems and clarify any confusion about them.

2. **Identification of Alternatives and Consequences:**
   In Step 2, group members help problem presenters explore the full range of choices available to them and the possible consequences of each choice.

3. **Decision, Action, and Evaluation:**
   In Step 3, problem presenters try to solve their target problems using the solutions they've identified, then report to the group on what happened and how effective it was in solving the target problems.

CHAPTER 10

The Three-Step
Problem-Solving Strategy

Most problems can't be solved in one group presentation. It usually takes between three and six sessions. So each problem has to be broken down into chunks that can be worked on in twenty to thirty minutes each session. The standard problem-solving strategy is designed to break the process down into pieces that make sense. There are three main steps: (1) Problem Identification and Clarification; (2) Identification of Alternatives and Consequences; and (3) Decision, Action, and Evaluation.

The process starts in the Agenda-Setting portion of the session, when group members volunteer to present problems or issues to be worked on in group. Whoever is bringing up a problem or issue at the moment is called the **problem presenter**. The rest of the group participates by asking questions and giving feedback. The next three chapters will go into detail on the questioning process. But first, here's an overview of the three main steps of problem solving.

Step 1: Problem Identification and Clarification

When problem presenters **identify** their problems, they answer the question "What is the problem and how is it affecting you?" At this stage the problem usually sounds vague and general. The problem presenter knows that something is wrong but can't clearly explain what it is. The process of clearly explaining the nature of the problem leads naturally into **clarification**.

55

A good clarifying strategy is to ask the problem presenter to tell the story of the problem, with a beginning, a middle, and an end. The story includes how this problem came up in the past and how it's likely to come up in the future. By listening carefully to these stories, leaders and group members can often hear sides of the problem that would otherwise remain hidden.

The problem identification and clarification process might take two group sessions. In the first session the problem presenter identifies the problem then answers several questions about it. The answers typically show that the problem presenter is confused about the problem and not really sure what's going on. The other group members usually point out this confusion in their feedback.

Sometimes the problem presenter will find that the questions and answers are bringing up difficult or painful emotions—anger, fear, sadness, worry, etc. These are sometimes called "hot responses." Hot responses are strong thoughts, feelings, or action urges that come up unexpectedly. When people are having hot responses, their stress rises above level 7. As you might remember from the "Reactions to Last Session" exercise, we measure stress levels on a scale from one to ten. At level 7 people "space out"; at level 8 they get defensive; at level 9 they overreact; and at level 10 they can't function—and they might get violent.

There are many ways to tell when your stress has risen above level 7. You might be finding it hard to concentrate on what you're saying or to understand what others are saying. You might feel hot or flushed, or feel the blood rushing in your veins. You might start to get very angry, sad, or scared. You might have a "fight or flight" response—an overwhelming urge to hit or yell at someone, or to run out of the room. You might feel like you can't move or speak. These are just a few examples of high-stress reactions.

People who feel these strong feelings and reactions coming up have a responsibility to tell the group that something's going on with them. They can do this by using the "time-out" signal—one arm crossed over an upright hand to make a "T." That tells the rest of the group members that it's time to stop asking questions for a few minutes. Then they need to go through a relaxation exercise to lower their stress levels. That way, they can get back on track and let the feelings help them in the problem-solving process. The relaxation exercise, and the other group members' responsibilities, are described in the next chapter.

After the questioning and feedback sessions, the group leader and the problem presenter work together to decide on an assignment that will help clarify the problem. This often involves writing a problem statement or interviewing other group members who have had similar problems. In the second group session the problem is presented again. This time the problem presenter can usually clarify the problem well enough to start looking at alternative solutions.

Step 2: Identifying Alternatives and Consequences

The second step of problem solving is identifying alternatives and consequences. Skilled problem presenters can usually identify at least three different ways of solving the problem, ways that have a good chance of working. These possible solutions are called **alternatives**. The problem presenter and other group members go through a questioning process that helps them think of several solutions that might work. The problem presenter should write a list of the alternative solutions identified during the session.

Each alternative will produce different **consequences** if the problem presenter tries to use it. Although no one can predict exactly what will happen, group members can use logical thinking to sort out the possible benefits and dangers of each alternative. This might take the form of an assignment for the problem presenter—taking each alternative solution and identifying the best, the worst, and the most likely things that might happen as a result.

The process of identifying alternatives and consequences usually takes two or three group sessions. In the first session the group helps the problem presenter start writing a list of alternative solutions. Then the group leader gives the problem presenter an assignment to interview at least three other people who have had similar problems and write down what those people have done to solve their problems.

In the second session the problem presenter brings back a completed list of alternative solutions. Then the group begins to ask questions about the logical consequences of using each alternative. Generally the group can easily point out the alternative solutions that are likely to fail. These are usually based on irrational thinking and self-defeating behavior that would make the problem worse rather than better. Often this self-defeating behavior is a long-standing habit for the problem presenter. These failed alternatives need to be pointed out and crossed off the list. Then the group helps the problem presenter identify the best three alternatives. The problem presenter is given the assignment of projecting the best, worst, and most likely outcomes of those three alternative solutions. To "project" an outcome is to imagine or predict what might happen.

In the third session the group explores the three logical consequences that the problem presenter has projected. Then the problem presenter is ready to move into the next step of problem solving.

Step 3: Decision, Action, and Evaluation

The third and final step involves decision, action, and evaluation. With this information the problem presenter has to decide which alternative solution to use.

Then the problem presenter must take action. The first step is to try to solve the problem by using the identified alternative. The next step is to evaluate the outcome, to see if the alternative worked. Even when problems are carefully thought through, the chosen alternative doesn't always work. If the alternative fails, it's crossed off the list and a new alternative is chosen.

It usually takes at least two or three sessions to finish the decision, action, and evaluation steps of problem solving. In the first session the problem presenter decides what alternatives to use and gives a detailed plan for carrying out that decision. Often the group leader will use mental rehearsal or role-playing techniques to give the problem presenter a chance to practice solving the problem in group before trying it in the real world.

The problem presenter might also have an assignment to practice the solution in a safe environment before trying it for real. One example of this kind of assignment might be expressing anger to a close friend or a recovery group sponsor before going home and trying to express anger to a spouse. The problem presenter would (1) have the practice session with the sponsor; (2) come to the second group session and report on how the practice assignment went; (3) talk about any concerns that still remain; and (4) have an assignment to try the solution for real. In the third group the problem presenter would report on how well the alternative worked in the real-life situation.

This table gives a quick look at how the group problem-solving process works and how it unfolds over a series of sessions.

Group #	Group Action	Assignment
Step 1: Problem Identification and Clarification		
Group #1	Present the problem and answer clarifying questions	Write a clarified problem statement
Group #2	Present the clarified problem to group	Write a list of alternative solutions
Step 2: Identify Alternatives and Consequences		
Group #3	Present alternative solutions and start identifying consequences	Interview three people who have solved similar problems
Group #4	Review the alternatives and select the best three	Project the best, worst, and most likely outcome of the three alternatives
Step 3: Decision, Action, and Evaluation		
Group #5	Select the best alternative and discuss or practice implementation	Practice the alternative in a safe and low-risk setting
Group #6	Report on problems and progress with practice sessions	Use the alternative in a real-life situation
Group #7	Report on outcome	

At first this might sound like a long and frustrating problem-solving process. But every step of this process is absolutely necessary if group members are going to learn to solve their problems for good. People usually enter group therapy because they have poor problem-solving skills (they don't know how to solve problems) and poor impulse control (they don't think things through before they act). They also often have poor self-discipline (they do what they want, when they want to, instead of following orderly processes that work). Many people also have a hard time learning from past experience. They create messes in their lives and never stop to think about what they did that caused those messes.

As you can see, this problem-solving process answers all of these issues by forcing group members to: (1) think things through before they act; (2) control their impulse to act out without thinking first; (3) evaluate what happened as a result of their past actions; and (4) think about possible consequences before they act. In other words, they're forced to start learning from their experiences.

During a typical problem-solving segment of a single group session, two or three members will work on solving their presenting problems. Each person will work for twenty to forty minutes. The group leader usually gives the problem presenter between ten and fifteen minutes to present the problem and answer the other group members' questions. Then the other group members give their feedback. When all members have given their feedback, the leader summarizes that feedback. Then the leader works with the problem presenter, creating an assignment that will move the problem-solving process into its next step.

By now you might be curious about how the other group members' questioning and feedback can really help the problem presenter work through serious life issues. The next chapter ("The Role of the Questioner") focuses on responsibilities in the questioning and feedback process, and where that process might go off track. Chapter 12 ("How to Ask Questions") goes into detail on the kinds of questions to ask and more effective ways of listening.

Chapter 13 ("Focusing Questions on Problem-Solving Steps") helps you tailor your questions to each of the three steps of problem solving.

The Role of the Questioner

Keep Your Role Clear:
- Don't talk about yourself.
- Don't give advice.
- Don't "footprint."

Manage "Hot Responses":
- Help problem presenters recognize that their behavior has changed.
- Ask them to breathe slowly and deeply.
- Help them connect with a safe place inside.
- Help them lower their stress.
- Help them identify the trigger.
- Don't try to take away their feelings.

Stay on Track:
- Point out when they've gotten off track.
- Ask them to remember their target problem.

Give Appropriate Feedback in the Feedback Session:
- "I think your problem is..."
- "My feelings about you as a person are..."

CHAPTER 11

The Role of the Questioner

If the problem presenter is honest, open-minded, and willing to work, the problem-solving process can bring about real break-throughs in painful or upsetting life problems. But believe it or not, the problem presenter isn't the one who gets the most out of the process.

The general rule is that the problem presenter gets 20 percent of the benefit and the other group members get 80 percent. Why? Because the other group members are practicing a way of thinking, asking questions, and looking honestly at problems that can be life saving when they apply it to their own problems. If your group is working on this model, you'll find yourself taking what you've learned in group and using it in many areas of life. You'll realize that you're thinking about your problems in new ways. The role of the questioner is a valuable one. Here are a few things you'll need to know in order to fill that role effectively.

Keep Your Role Clear

The role of the questioner is unique. You're there to help problem presenters find and speak their truth—just by asking questions. There are many other things you might be tempted to do. You'll be asked to become aware of those temptations and resist them. Here are some common ways of going outside the questioner's role, ways that can be harmful to the problem presenter or the group process.

You might be tempted to start talking about yourself or about problems you've had and solutions that have worked or not worked for you. That would put the whole questioning process off track. At that point the group's attention is no longer on the problem presenter; it's on you. It might be that hearing about your experience will help the problem presenter. But if that's true, it will help just as much if you talk about it while you're the problem presenter. You can't be both presenter and questioner at once.

You also might be tempted to give advice. That would be a mistake for several reasons. First, the goal of questioning is to find out information and clarify it, not to tell or suggest things for the problem presenter to do. If you give advice, most people get defensive and don't take it anyway. Even if they do take it, a solution that would work well for you might turn out to be wrong for them. And it's much more important for the problem presenter to learn how to solve problems effectively than it is to find the "best" solution for this particular problem. If you come up with the solution, it will rob the presenter of the chance to grapple with the problem and learn from it.

You can always convert a statement of advice into a question or a series of questions. For example, if you want to say, "You should go to more Twelve-Step meetings," you can turn that advice into one or more questions: "How many Twelve-Step meetings do you go to each week? Are they helpful to you in working on this issue? Do you think it would help you to go to more meetings? Have you ever considered using a Twelve-Step program to deal with this problem?" These kinds of questions can lead people to consider the solutions you want them to consider. But because they figured the solutions out for themselves as a response to your questions, they're better able to accept them, take ownership of them, and put them to work in their lives.

If you do that, though, be careful to avoid another common temptation: to use questions that lead people to see their problems as you see them, even if you're wrong about them. Their problems might be quite different from anything you've seen or experienced, and your line of questioning might lead people away from understanding what their true problems are. This is called **footprinting,** because you leave a "footprint" in someone else's mind—the mark of your own opinions and experiences. If you have an opinion about the nature of someone's problem, save it for the feedback part of the problem-solving session. That way you can make it clear that it's your opinion, and the problem presenter can decide to take it or leave it.

Manage Hot Responses

Sometimes problem presenters will be working on problems that have been causing them a lot of pain, fear, worry, or anger. At other times they might be working on problems that seem matter-of-fact, but something they say, hear, or think will bring up strong painful or upsetting emotions and urges. They might get angry, defensive, or fearful, or start crying. As discussed in the last chapter, these kinds of reactions are called **hot responses**. Hot responses are valuable because they can point toward the center of the problem. They also give people a chance to feel their emotions in a safe and caring setting.

Hot responses have to be managed, though. This means that the group helps problem presenters become aware of the hot responses, then lower their stress levels so they can think clearly and learn from the emotions they're feeling. If group members show symptoms of stress levels of seven or higher (spacing out, getting defensive, overreacting, getting violent, etc.), other group members need to take responsibility for helping them manage their responses.

The first step is to ask, "Are you aware that your behavior has changed?" Clarifying questions might be a good follow-up, including "What do you think is happening?" or "What's different now than a few minutes ago?" It's important to use active listening when people answer these questions. Then take action to help them lower their stress. Use the **Immediate Relaxation Response**, an exercise much like the one your group leader uses at the beginning of the Reactions to Last Session.

Let them know you're going to use a relaxation technique to get their stress level below a seven. Ask them to sit straight in their chair, feet on the floor, hands resting comfortably. In a calm voice, ask them to take a slow, deep breath; hold it for a few seconds; then let it out slowly. Continue to ask them to breathe in this way. Ask them to get in touch with an idea, a vision, or a part of themselves that helps them feel safe and whole. Do this until they report that their stress is back down below level 7. Then ask them what triggered their response and the thoughts and beliefs that might have been behind their feelings.

If other people's painful or upsetting emotions make you uncomfortable, you might be tempted to try to take their emotions away—by hugging, touching, or telling them it will turn out all right; relieving their fears or sadness; convincing them they shouldn't be angry; etc. If you're a compassionate person, this can be a strong temptation, but don't give in to it. Whatever they're feeling, they need to feel it right now. They'll live through it, and it will help them in their healing process. It's not okay to get violent in group, but it *is* okay to have strong emotions. Don't take away people's opportunity to grow through their pain and upset.

Stay on Track

It's very important to keep the questions focused on the target problem. But sometimes talking about the target problem will feel scary or uncomfortable for the problem presenter. The presenter might avoid dealing with the target problem by going off on an interesting line of thought that has nothing to do with the problem being presented. If at any time you're not sure what the target problem is, you're probably off track. You can get back on track by asking "We seem to be getting off track. Could you tell me again what the target problem is that we're working on?"

Sometimes when you're going in the right direction with your questions, the problem presenter will get anxious or uncomfortable with the focus of the questioning and just stop talking. If that happens, don't stop asking questions or change your direction. You might be on to something important. If you're afraid you're getting too pushy, or afraid you might have hurt the problem presenter's feelings, ask whether you should stop or keep going.

Give Appropriate Feedback in the Feedback Session

After all group members have asked their questions, each member will get a chance to give feedback to the problem presenter, answering two questions: (1) "What's your understanding of the problem this person is working on?"; and (2) "After listening to the problem presenter work on this problem, how do you feel about him/her as a person?" The leader will often ask you to give feedback by completing two statements: (1) "I think your problem is..."; and (2) "My feelings about you as a person are...".

As you get better at giving feedback, the leader might also ask you to tell the problem presenter about the strengths and challenges you see in him or her. You can do this by finishing two statements: (1) "The strengths I see that will help you solve this problem are..."; and (2) "The challenges I see that might get in the way of your solving the problem are...".

You'll have only one or two minutes to give your feedback, so you'll need to learn how to get to the point, say what you mean, then move on. It's important to remember that group time is limited, and the group can't spend all its time on one person's problem. It's also important to remember that the person receiving the feedback has limits, too. People can only process a little information at a time. Feedback that's short, clear, and to the point is more likely to be remembered and used.

So as you can see, the role of the questioner carries many responsibilities. The next two chapters go into detail on the questioning process. Once you've read those chapters and had a chance to practice the skills, you'll be in an excellent position to carry out these responsibilities. You'll be able to help others while you change your whole approach to problem solving.

How to Ask Questions

Use Active Listening:
- Ask a question.
- Listen to the answer.
- Tell the person what you heard, using same-word feedback and paraphrasing.
- Ask the person whether or not you heard it correctly.

Use Open-Ended, Closed, and Focus Questions Appropriately:
- Use open-ended questions to get more information.
- Use closed questions to confirm specific information.
- Use focus questions to help the person make choices.

Clarify Thoughts, Feelings, Urges, Actions, and Relationships:
- "Tell me about the problem."
- "When you experience that problem, what do you tend to think?"
- "When you're thinking that way, what do you tend to feel?"
- "When you feel that way, what do you have an urge to do?"
- "When you feel the urge to do that, what do you actually do?"
- "When you do that, how does it affect your relationships?"
- "Can you think of another way to cope with the problem?"

CHAPTER 12

How to Ask Questions

Asking effective problem-solving questions isn't as easy as it sounds. Group time is limited, and members need to make every word count. This chapter gives clear guidelines for asking questions that will truly be of help to all group members.

Use Active Listening

Effective listening is the most important part of the questioning process. When you ask questions in group, you'll learn to use active listening. Active listening is a method designed to make sure you've really heard and understood the problem presenter's answers correctly, and to let the problem presenter know that you've heard and understood. Active listening has four parts: asking a question, listening to the answer, telling the problem presenter what you heard, and finding out if you heard it correctly.

The first step is to **ask a question** that's useful in solving the problem. Useful questions are clear, relevant, and intelligent. A *clear* question is easy to understand. A *relevant* question is directly related to the problem. An *intelligent* question makes sense and gives the person answering a new way of thinking about or looking at the problem.

It's important to look straight at the problem presenter when you're asking questions. That gives the problem presenter a chance to feel connected to you, and to feel seen and heard. If the problem presenter isn't looking at you when you ask a question, it's okay to say something like, "Could you look at me for a moment?"

The second step of active listening is to **listen to the answer**. Many people ask a question, then start thinking right away about the next question before they hear the answer to the first one. They shoot off a string of questions, leaving the problem presenter feeling interrogated instead of understood. You can avoid this by listening carefully to each answer.

The third step is to **tell the problem presenter what you heard**. You do this using two techniques: *same-word feedback* and *paraphrasing*.

When you use same-word feedback, you tell people what you heard them say, using the same words they used. This helps people feel listened to ("You heard me"), understood ("You know what I mean"), taken seriously ("You think I'm important"), and affirmed ("You're on my side").

Let's say, for example, a woman in group has said, "I'm sick of the way my husband acts when I come home from my Twelve-Step meetings. He asks me all kinds of questions about the men in the group and how they treat me. Then he tells me I don't need to go to so many meetings." Same-word feedback for that might be: "I heard you say that you're sick of the way your husband acts when you get home from your Twelve-Step meetings. He asks a lot of questions about the men in the group and how they treat you. Then he tells you that you don't need to go to so many meetings."

One warning: same-word feedback might be annoying to you at first. It might feel silly to repeat what someone just said. But the reality is that it's very easy to hear someone wrong, even if you're listening carefully. Many tragic misunderstandings have been based on one or two words heard wrong. So while you're learning the skill of same-word feedback, you'll need to use it all the time to get used to it. Then after you get comfortable with the skill, you can save it for the most important points that the person is making.

Same-word feedback sets up that common understanding that lets you take the next step, paraphrasing. When you paraphrase, you repeat what you heard the problem presenter say, using different words but sticking to the same meaning. A paraphrasing of the problem quoted above might be, "What I'm hearing you say is that your husband is very jealous and you're tired of the way he tries to control you." Paraphrasing helps you make sure you understand the problem in your own words. It also can help the problem presenter see the situation in a new way. Like same-word feedback, skillful paraphrasing can help the problem presenter feel listened to, understood, taken seriously, and affirmed as a person. But it's important to avoid footprinting, especially in the paraphrasing process.

The fourth step is to **find out whether or not you heard it correctly**. Ask the problem presenter, "Did I understand you correctly?" or "Did I get it right?" This step is absolutely necessary to respect the problem presenter's experience and make sure you're both working on the same problem. Often when you ask for confirmation like this, it's followed by an intense conversation between you and the problem presenter. This conversation is at the heart of the problem-solving process.

Use Open-Ended, Closed, and Focus Questions Appropriately

There are three kinds of questions, open-ended, closed, and focus. **An open-ended question** is one that can't logically be answered by a yes or no answer. These kinds of questions are used for getting more information. **A closed question** is one that asks for a yes or no answer. Sometimes people choose to answer closed questions with more than just yes or no, but you can't count on it. Closed questions are best used for getting the person to agree or disagree with specific points. **Focus questions** are used to help people make choices.

Most of the time you'll be asking questions to get more information. So in group you'll usually need to ask open-ended questions. For example, the closed question "Are you married?" isn't likely to get much more than "yes" or "no" out of the person who's answering it. But you can turn it into an opened-ended question by saying, "Tell me what your current love relationship is like." You'll get a lot more information that way.

Closed questions are useful when you need to hear the problem presenter confirm or deny specific information—tell you whether or not that information is true, or whether or not you've paraphrased correctly. For example, after the problem presenter has described the relationship, you might ask the closed question, "Are you saying that alcohol and drugs have caused problems in your marriage?" This forces the problem presenter to make a commitment to a definite and specific answer.

A focus question is one that helps people clarify their viewpoints. It's used when they've presented two conflicting points of view and you're not sure which one is correct. You ask the person to focus: "I heard you say you don't mind it when your girlfriend asks you to watch her kids, then I also heard you say you sometimes get angry when she does that. Which one is accurate? Is it that you don't mind or that it sometimes makes you angry?"

Focus questions are very useful when people have inner conflicts. One "part" of them says one thing and another "part" says something else. By identifying both of their conflicting thoughts, you can help them decide which thoughts are correct.

Clarify Thoughts, Feelings, Actions, and Relationships

As you might remember from the first section of this book, an important skill in problem solving is the ability to understand and connect thoughts, feelings, urges, actions, and relationships. You can help the problem presenter do this through the questions you ask. In the following example we've highlighted these kinds of questions by taking out the same-word feedback and the paraphrasing that would ordinarily be combined with this process. Here are the clarifying questions alone:

Questioner: Could you tell me about the problem you want to work on?

Problem Presenter: The problem is that every time I get a paycheck I feel the urge to start using cocaine.

Questioner: When was the last time this happened?

Problem Presenter: It happened last Friday when I got paid.

Questioner: Just what happened?

Problem Presenter: I picked up the paycheck, and as I started walking out of the building I started thinking about how good it would feel to get some cocaine.

Questioner: Can you remember exactly what you started to think?

Problem Presenter: Yes. I started thinking that I had a lot of cash. I worked hard for it, and I deserved some good times. I had enough money to spend a little of it on cocaine. It would help me feel better and have a good time.

Questioner: When you're thinking that way, what are you feeling?

Problem Presenter: I'm not sure.

Questioner: Think about it for a minute. Which of these words sounds closest to what you're feeling? Are you mad? sad? glad? or scared?

Problem Presenter: I guess the word "mad." I feel angry because I can't use cocaine. It's the only thing I know how to do to turn off the stress and have a good time.

Questioner: When you're feeling that way, what do you have an urge to do?

Problem Presenter: I want to use cocaine!

Questioner: What do you actually do?

Problem Presenter: I go home determined not to use, and I sweat it out.

Questioner: When you go home feeling like that, how does it affect your relationship with your wife?

Problem Presenter: Sometimes I get mad at little things she does that wouldn't bother me if I weren't mad already. We usually end up getting in a fight.

Questioner: Do you ever go home and tell her you're struggling with an urge to use cocaine?

Problem Presenter: No! She's still mad from when I used to use before. If I told her I was fighting off an urge to use, she'd go off on me!

Problem Presenter: Can you think of any way besides using cocaine that you can get rid of the stress, feel good, and have a good time?

Again, in an actual questioning process you'd be using same-word feedback and paraphrasing. But notice how the questions are arranged:

- "Tell me about the problem."
- "When you experience that problem, what do you tend to think?"
- "When you're thinking that way, what do you tend to feel?"
- "When you feel that way, what do you have an urge to do?"
- "When you feel the urge to do that, what do you actually do?"
- "When you do that, how does it affect your relationships?"
- "Can you think of another way to cope with the problem?"

This line of questioning helps people see how their thoughts lead to feelings, which lead to urges, which lead to actions, which affect their relationships. In other words, they start seeing how their problems develop.

Clarify the Language of Problem Presentation

Problem presenters will sometimes state their problems in words that help keep them from understanding what the problem really is. As a questioner, one of your goals is to help clarify these kinds of statements. Three examples are generalizations, deletions, and distortions.

A **generalization** is a statement that's all-inclusive, like "Everything is going wrong!" You can challenge this by asking clarifying questions: "What do you mean everything is going wrong? Can you be more specific and give us an example of exactly what's going wrong?"

A **deletion** is a statement that fails to give all the information that's needed. For example, a group member might say, "I got angry." This statement is incomplete because it doesn't explain who the problem presenter got angry at, what the person did that led to the anger, and how the problem presenter acted out the anger. You can challenge this by asking the clarifying questions, "Who did you get angry with? What did they do that caused you to get angry? What did you do after you got angry?"

A **distortion** is a statement that blows something out of proportion or gets the facts wrong. Distortions often involve words that aren't accurate or helpful in solving a problem. The problem presenter might say "He blew me away!" Now, the problem presenter wasn't really blown away, but it's clear that the other person said or did something that led to some kind of strong emotional reaction. You can help clarify the problem by asking questions like, "What exactly did he do that blew you away?" and "How did you feel when you felt like you were being blown away?"

If all this sounds like a lot to remember, don't worry. You'll have plenty of time to learn and practice these listening and questioning skills in group. There are a lot of skills to learn and they won't all come at once. But even your first attempts to use them will be helpful–to you and to the problem presenter. And as you start using these skills on your own problems, you'll begin to find your problems much easier to solve.

Focusing Questions on Problem-Solving Steps

Step 1: Problem Identification and Clarification

1a: Problem Identification
  - What is the problem and how is it affecting you?

1b: Problem Clarification
  - Who, what, when, why, and how?
  - A story, with a beginning, middle, and end.
  - How this relates to the target problem and to other problems.

Step 2: Identifying Alternatives and Consequences

2a: Identifying Alternatives
  - Solutions that have been tried.
  - What worked and what didn't?
  - Other alternatives.

2b: Identifying the Consequences of Each Alternative
  - The benefits and disadvantages of each alternative.
  - The best, worst, and most likely outcomes.

Step 3: Decision, Action, and Evaluation

3a: Decision
  - Alternatives to try, steps to take, when to do it.
  - People to involve, preparation and support needed.

3b: Action
  - Whether or not the action was taken.

3c: Evaluation
  - What was done, how well it worked, and the consequences.

CHAPTER 13

Focusing Questions on Problem-Solving Steps

This chapter gives examples of specific questions to ask in each of the steps or stages of problem solving. Please feel free to keep these pages in front of you when it's your turn to ask questions.

Step 1: Problem Identification and Clarification

1a: Problem Identification:
· What is the problem and how is it affecting you?

1b: Problem Clarification:
· Who is involved in this problem?
· What are you or other people doing to cause or complicate the problem?
· When did this problem first start?
· Why are you interested in solving the problem right now? (Why didn't you solve it yesterday or put it off until tomorrow?)
· How is this problem affecting you or other people?
· Describe the way this problem happened as if it were a story with a beginning, a middle, and an ending.
· Describe how this problem is likely to happen in the future.
· What other problems are there in your life that are like this problem or might be related to it?
· How does this problem relate to your target problem?
· Does this problem create an urge to relapse into the old behavior of your target problem?

- Does this problem make it harder for you to practice your program of recovery from your target problem?

Step 2: Identifying Alternatives and Consequences

2a: Identifying Alternatives:
- What ways have you used in the past to try to solve this problem?
- What was helpful? What was not helpful? What seemed to make things worse?
- What have other people with similar problems done to solve them?
- What new ideas can you think of to try to solve this problem?

2b: Identifying the Consequences of Each Alternative:
- What are the benefits and disadvantages of each alternative?
- Identify the three best alternative solutions.
- Analyze each of the top three alternatives by asking, "If I used this alternative..."
  > "...what's the best that could happen?"
  > "...what's the worst that could happen?"
  > "...what's the most likely thing that probably will happen?"

Step 3: Decision, Action, and Evaluation

3a: Decision:
- What alternatives do you plan to use to try to solve this problem?
- What steps will you take to put that solution into action?
- Who else needs to be involved in trying to solve this problem?
- When will you take action? (Name a specific date and time.)
- What kind of preparation and support do you need to put the solution to work?

3b: Action:
- Did you do it?

3c: Evaluation:

- What exactly did you do?
- How closely were you able to follow your original plan?
- How well did the attempted solution work?
- Was the problem solved, or do you need to try another alternative?

After you've used these kinds of questions for a while, they begin to become second nature for you. Combined with the questioning skills described in the last chapter, they can be a powerful tool for clarifying and solving the problems that trouble your own life.

CHAPTER 14
A Final Word

Now that you've read about your responsibilities and opportunities in Problem-Solving Group Therapy, you have all the information about the process that you'll need. Your group and your group leader can supply the rest—a chance to make these skills and insights come to life.

If you've been using this model for a while, you probably know about some of its benefits. You've probably found yourself changing in the way you face and solve your problems. We hope this *Group Member's Guide* will help you get even more out of the group therapy experience.

Many group members like to have the instructions easily available while they work in group. The group member's *Tool Kit* provides all the important rules, agendas, and instructions in a quick-reference format. There is also a set of posters that can be displayed in the room where your group meets. These posters put the rules and agendas up where you can see them while you work.

Your life will never be free of problems. But you can begin to solve the core target problems that have been causing pain and upset over and over in your life. You can trade those in for a better set of problems, and work on solving that set of problems, too.

When you learn the skills of problem solving with your group, problems become challenges that you have the resources to meet. You'll no longer feel like a victim of bad luck, confusion, and other people's unfair actions. You won't be problem free, but you will be free.

A Note to Group Leaders

Congratulations for choosing this innovative, powerful model of group therapy, a model that helps your clients quickly identify and solve problems, while it meets the needs of managed care organizations.

This book is your group members' counterpart to *A Group Leader's Guide to Brief Strategic Problem-Solving Group Therapy* by Terence T. Gorski. While the leader's guide goes into significant detail on procedures for running a group, this *Group Member's Guide* contains the information your participants will need to prepare themselves for full participation and a safe, rewarding group experience.

We recommend that each group member have a copy of this book to read outside of group sessions. It's structured so that its individual chapters can be used as assignments for group members. You can follow the sequence of chapters, or you can assign specific chapters to members who need to learn specific group skills.

The first few chapters make excellent preparation for group members who are new to this process. Even if members have had other group experiences, this model will surprise them, both in its procedures and in its effects. Though most members will be quite pleased with the outcome of participation in this model, a thorough preparation will give them greater confidence and willingness to participate.

Two other tools are also available to help group members maximize the effectiveness of their experience. One is the *Tool Kit* that contains handouts to cue members on the key points of important group procedures. Another is the set of wall posters that can give group members strong visual reminders.

These have proved valuable to members whose levels of stress, memory deficits, or lack of longevity in group can make it difficult to remember what's expected of them. We suggest that you reduce the amount of embarrassment these group members might feel by "normalizing" the use of these tools. You might encourage all group members to get out their tool kits at the beginning of group, and/ or place the posters in clear sight during sessions.

Additional training for group leaders is available through the CENAPS Corporation, 18650 Dixie Highway, Homewood, IL 60430 (phone: 708/799-5000). We would love to hear how this model is working for you and for your clients.

A Group LEADERS GUIDE to
Brief Strategic
PROBLEM-SOLVING GROUP THERAPY
Making Group Therapy Work in the Managed Care Environment

A "must read" for every serious group therapist. It includes:
 • The role of group therapy in the new era of chemical dependency and behavior health.
 • How to develop and implement targeted, strategic group treatment plans using a powerful integration of cognitive, behavioral, and experiential methods.
 • How to use group therapy methods to change irrational thoughts, unmanageable feelings, self-defeating behaviors, and dysfunctional relationships.
 • How to orient new members by using standard group responsibilities, group rules, and procedures for dealing with problem group members.
 • How to use an eight-step standard group therapy agenda.
 • How to use a standard three-step problem-solving process.

It will be a snap to start using problem-solving group therapy procedures immediately after reading this book.
17-026062

Group Therapy Tool Kit

(Companion to *Brief Strategic Problem-Solving Group Therapy: A Guide for Group Members*)

This tool kit contains reference copies of all the guidelines and procedures that group members will need to follow. Twelve handout sheets per kit. Sold in packages of 20 kits.
17-026084   (Pkg. of 20)

Poster Series

This set of fifteen posters contains reference displays of all the guidelines and procedures that group members will need to follow. 17" x 22"
17-026085   (Pkg. of 15)

To order: Call Herald House/Independence Press
1-800-767-8181 or (816) 252-5010
In Canada call 1-800-373-8382 or (519) 836-8982